DATE DUE			

POLISH JEWS: THE FINAL CHAPTER

POLISH JEWS: THE FINAL CHAPTER

text by
EARL VINECOUR

photographs by
CHUCK FISHMAN

NEW YORK • NEW YORK UNIVERSITY PRESS • 1977

Library of Congress Cataloging in Publication Data

Vinecour, Earl.
  Polish Jews: the final chapter

  Bibliography: p.
  1. Jews in Poland—Intellectual life. 2. Jews in Poland—Pictorial works.
3. Poland—Intellectual life. 4. Poland/Description and travel—Views.
I. Fishman, Charles. II. Title
                DS135.P6V47   943.8'004'924   77-83266
                        ISBN 0-8147-8756-8

V 782ρ

Acknowledgments

The authors give special thanks to Samuel Sorgenstein, a native of Warsaw, for his guidance and professional advice throughout the project, as well as for his meticulous translations of pertinent Polish-language material; to Jacqueline Alon, Folklore Research Center, Hebrew University, Jerusalem; and to Dr. C. William Horrell, Cinema and Photography Department, Southern Illinois University, Carbondale, Illinois.

In no other country than ancient Israel, have Jews lived continuously for as many centuries, in as large numbers, and with as much autonomy as in Poland. It is estimated that during the Middle Ages, eighty percent of all the Jews in the world lived there. By 1939, there were about 3,500,000 Jews living in Poland, ten percent of the country's total population, and forty percent of its urban.

For a thousand years, Jews played a key role in laying the foundations of Polish trade and industry. At the same time, they painstakingly developed, over the centuries, their own unique civilization, and they did so as nowhere else in the world, without apologies and without inhibitions. Theirs was a self-contained, yet all-pervasive world, a vast network of religious, social, and even political institutions; a kaleidoscope of cultural and artistic creativity, manifest in an indigenous architectural style, polychrome murals, wrought-iron and hammered-brass liturgical artifacts. It was in their own mother tongue that their many-sided talents overflowed into a voluminous Yiddish literature, vibrant press, and into the realms of music and theater. From roots sunk deep into the Polish soil for a millennium, blossomed a way of life where spiritual values and ideals blended into a folk culture, where kabbalistic mysticism and Talmudic rationality were inextricably interwoven. Bobov, Kotsk, Ger, Lublin were for them mystical utterances, rather than the names of Polish towns; paths to divinity through the gateways of Hasidic courts, rather than mere geographic locations. "The city of Lublin," wrote one Hasid, "is the land of Israel; the courtyard of our seer's *Bes Medrash* (House of Study), Jerusalem; the *Bes Medrash*, itself, the mount of the Holy Temple; the seer's quarters, the Temple court; the seer's room, the Holy of Holies, and from the seer's mouth speaks the *Shekinah* (Holy Spirit)."

The *shtetlekh* (Jewish rural communities) of Poland were immortalized by such Yiddish writers as Scholem Aleichem, Mendele Mokher Seforim and Isaac L. Peretz, as places where Torah had been studied from time immemorial; where in spite of poverty and squalor, practically all the inhabitants were Biblical scholars; where the synagogues and houses of study reverberated to the chants of Talmudic *pilpul* (disputation), the parables and aphorisms of sages, as well as the witticisms and comic legends of folk humor; where each day at twilight, tailors and copper-smiths, innkeepers and beggars would gather around tables to listen to discourses on the great books of law, to interpretations of Scripture, to readings from ethical writings; and where on the Sabbaths and festive occasions, the entire community would unite in dancing and singing, their voices interweaving in melodious sounds whereby the soul of the universe seemed to join in the contagious merriment.

Thirty years have now passed since the doors to Jewish life in Poland were slammed shut at Auschwitz, Treblinka, Sobibor, Chelmno. Yet in the shadows of this one-thousand-year-old, lost world, what, if anything, has survived?

Jews first came to Poland from Byzantium and the Moslem East before the Slavonic tribes of the area united to create a Polish kingdom in the tenth century. The discovery in Wronki in 1920 of a one-thousand-year-old synagogue provided evidence of thriving Jewish commercial settlements in Poland a generation before the arrival of Christianity. Among the earliest Polish coins to be found are many bearing Hebrew inscriptions, attesting to the fact that the Jews had obtained the royal franchise for operating the country's mint.

Streams of Jewish immigrants headed east to Poland from all over the rest of Europe as the flames of bigotry were fanned by the crusaders. The immigrations became a flood in the fourteenth century, when the Polish King, Casimir the Great, in order to develop his kingdom's vast untapped resources, encouraged Jewish settlement by extending unprecedented privileges to Jews. His charter represented one of the most humane systems of laws ever enacted regarding minorities. Jews were granted virtual self-government and total religious and cultural autonomy. Jews were not to be confined to ghettoes, as elsewhere in Europe, nor were they obliged to pay discriminatory taxes, or restricted in choice of occupation; they were subject only to their own laws, and free from all ecclesiastical and municipal rule. They were also given the right to bear arms and absolute freedom of worship. These privileges of Casimir were ratified by successive kings throughout Polish history, creating a unique environment for the unparalleled growth and flourishing of Jewish heritage and culture.

The autonomy which Polish kings encouraged enabled Jews to build a communal structure which touched upon every aspect of life. Theirs was a world in which Talmudic law was not relegated, as in the West, merely to religious ritual, but operated in the marketplace and streets as well.

Each separate Jewish community was administered by its *kahal*, a committee of scholars and oligarchs, and all the *kahals* were subject to a national legislative body known as the Council of Four Lands. Modeled after the *Sejm* (Polish National Diet), the Council was the only Jewish parliament that ever existed outside of Israel and was unparalleled in Jewish history for its duration and for the size of the territory its jurisdiction covered. The Council was backed by the authority of the Polish crown and was officially referred to as the *Congressus Judaicus*. It had a decisive influence over every aspect of Polish-Jewish life from 1592 until its demise in 1764.

The *kahals* and the Council maintained a complex system of synagogues, study houses, courts of law, hospitals, schools, welfare programs, and even tax collecting.

In the arena of Polish politics, however, there were other factors at play besides the expediency of kings intent on the economic development of their kingdom, and the struggles in that arena had a marked effect upon Polish Jewish history.

Poland had been one of Europe's first constitutional monarchies: not only was the power of the throne balanced by the *szlachta*, an oligarchical nobility, but other sectors of society, notably the German burghers—the Jews' fiercest competitors, who, like them, enjoyed special privileges—and the Catholic Church with its vested interests in landed property exercised considerable power.

The tensions inherent in the interrelationships of these power groups formed a paradigm of Polish-Jewish history. Generally, when the *szlachta* and throne were stable, Jewish affairs flourished. When the Germans and the Church gained power, anti-Semitism increased. The Church, especially, saw anti-Semitism as its most effective tool in seeking to weaken the economic power of secular authority. Catholic synods were constantly passing anti-Jewish laws, but the Polish kings just as steadfastly prevented their enactment. The throne was far too wise economically to be swayed by ecclesiastical Machiavellianism; thus it was only the power of the Polish kings and nobility that made Poland the safest place for Jews in Europe for many centuries.

External factors also played a decisive role in Polish-Jewish history. Poland had the misfortune of being squeezed by three predatory, expansionistic neighbors—Russia to the east, Germany to the west, Austria to the south—each one engaging in repeated incursions of her borders.

In 1648 a major disaster overwhelmed Poland and especially the Jews. Ukrainian peasants in the east rebelled against Polish rule and, in an ensuing orgy of sadism, 200,000 Jews were murdered and 700 communities totally wiped out. This tragedy was a determining factor in the subsequent rise in Poland of the greatest religious revival in Jewish history—the Hasidic movement.

In the latter part of the eighteenth century, Poland was partitioned by her neighbors. During that period, many Jews combined forces with Polish patriots to free their country from foreign domination. One of those Jews, Colonel Berek Joselewicz, became a Polish national hero fighting with the legendary Tadeusz Kosciuszko, who later joined the revolutionary army of George Washington in America's struggle for independence. Of the Jewish participation in Poland's national struggle, Kosciuszko wrote: "The Jews have proven to the world that when the

welfare of humanity is at stake, they know not how to spare their lives."
Rabbis delivered patriotic speeches urging support for the national
struggle against Russia. Prayers were offered at High Holiday services for
the success of the insurrections. However, the struggles for power within
the arena of Polish politics continued to generate anti-Semitism.

The nineteenth century found Poland in the throes of industrial-
ization and urbanization, with the rise of a Polish middle class and growth
of a proletariat drawn from a previously overwhelming agrarian society.
Gradually, key economic positions held by Jews for centuries were being
contested for by Poles, resulting in competition that spurred increasing
anti-Semitism. Sporadic violence and excesses led to large-scale emigration. For the first time the flood tide of Jews to Poland, begun under
Casimir the Great in the fourteenth century, began to turn. So many Jews
left Poland for America, that today the majority of American Jews are of
Polish origin.

Those who remained were faced with "Polonization," a campaign for displacing Jews from the economy, not through normal
competition, but through boycotts, discrimination, and violence. The
Jews had done their job too well. Over the centuries, they had transformed Poland from an underdeveloped, backward country into a com-
mercially and industrially viable nation. They had tapped her natural
resources, established her textile industry and other industrial and
commercial enterprises, and laid the very foundations of her economy. In
so doing they were rewarded with the country's contempt, and the
government now viewed them as obsolete. By 1939 one third of Poland's
Jews were dependent upon American Jewish relief agencies for their
survival; and when Hitler conquered Poland, he found every Polish
political party, with the sole exception of the Socialists, committed to
anti-Semitism.

The Jews of Poland at the hands of the Nazis suffered the
greatest holocaust in history. From 1939 to 1945, ninety percent of them
were brutally slaughtered. The Poles who aided Jews during those hellish

years were the exception rather than the rule. Less than one percent of the Polish Jews were saved by Poles during the war years, the smallest percentage of Jews saved by citizens in any country under Nazi rule.

After the defeat of the Nazis, the Polish Jews who had survived, either by fleeing to the USSR, or by hiding in caves and forests, sought to re-establish themselves again in Poland, and to restore their shattered thousand-year-old heritage. The post-war Communist government even encouraged and aided them, so that by 1946, 250,000 Jews were living there. Returning Jews, however, met hostility from Poles who, in their absence, had appropriated their property, homes, and businesses. Violent excesses broke out here and there. On July 4, 1946, the largest anti-Jewish outbreaks since the defeat of the Nazis, claimed forty-two Jewish lives in Kielce. The police did not interfere. Subsequently, hundreds of Jews, survivors of the holocaust, perished in violent attacks throughout Poland, which finally convinced the majority of Polish Jews that emigration was the only option left open to them.

Following the complete Stalinization of the post-war regime in 1948, only about 70,000 Jews remained in the country. Internal power struggles and the fact of Soviet domination combined to generate a continuous anti-Semitism, despite the fact that the Jews had been reduced to an insignificant percentage of the population—an anti-Semitism, if you will, without Jews.

Labor unrest caused by stringent economic conditions, combined with inherent Polish nationalism, burst forth in the 1950's and 60's into open demonstrations, culminating in widespread student riots in 1968, sparked by a government's ban of a nineteenth-century anti-Russian play by Adam Mickiewicz, Poland's illustrious poet. The pro-Soviet government sought to turn popular unrest away from Soviet domination by employing the traditional Polish scapegoat, this time clothed in the Communist language of anti-Zionism. A wide-spread campaign was thus unleashed in the mass media blaming Zionism for all of Poland's ills. Inflammatory speeches by party leaders, carried by radio and television, harangued against alleged Zionist conspiracies. Most of the Jews who could leave the country during those turbulent years, did so. By the summer of 1975, even as the anti-Zionist smokescreen began to dissipate, the condition of the remaining Jews was shrouded in mystery. What had become of all the synagogues, historic cemeteries, and communal institutions that had been so painstakingly built up over many generations and had miraculously survived the holocaust? What was the situation of those who were living out the last chapter of a thousand-year-old saga?

A clear answer to these questions obviously meant the arduous task of touring the country, not an easy undertaking given the political climate. Armed only with historical perspective and cameras, we entered Poland in the summer of 1975, appearing to be American college students on vacation. By the end of two months, we had traveled to nearly a hundred cities and towns, spoken to countless people, and recorded what remained of what was once the world's most vibrant Jewish community.

We found that the Jewish population, composed now mostly of the elderly and indigent, had disappeared from all but a few centers. Everywhere, however, were to be seen crumbling, decayed synagogues and communal buildings, some of which had been converted to other uses; neglected Jewish cemeteries and monuments, and thousands of tombstones scattered about, transforming Poland into the world's largest Jewish burial ground.

Of all the cities in Poland, only Cracow was found to have a considerable percentage of its historic synagogues and institutional buildings survive the ravages of Nazism intact. The city's major synagogues—about one hundred—had been concentrated in the Kazimierz quarter, the former heart of the ancient Jewish community. Today, on almost every street there are to be found former synagogues, study houses or schools, which either have been converted to other uses or stand in abandon. The famous High Synagogue, built in 1663, is still there, but it is now used as an apartment house. Formerly, it contained

1. Cracow.
Fourteenth-century *Alte Shul*,
Poland's oldest existing synagogue.
The parapet of bricks and stone,
decorated with blind arcades,
shows the influence of the
style of the medieval castles of the
Cracow nobility.

some unique murals which, contrary to traditional antirepresentational proscriptions, showed Biblical figures in complete form. There is the Isaac Jakubowicz synagogue, named after the banker of King Wladislaw IV, under whose royal patronage the lofty edifice, with its windows set high in the lunettes, was constructed in 1640. Today, it is used as a warehouse. The famous Hebrew secondary school building on Brzozowa Street remains, but it now houses a technical college. Many synagogues and study houses still stand on Jozefa Street, but they have been converted into private homes. One, however, at number 42, still maintains the Hebrew inscriptions and stars of David over its entrance. The renowned Cracow Yeshiva still stands on Esther Street, but is totally abandoned. Inside, on the walls, can be seen the fading memorial plaques dedicated to those who, over the years, made donations to its upkeep.

Of all the synagogues remaining in the Kazimierz quarter, only the *Alte Shul* on Szeroka Street has been restored by the government. It is

2. Cracow. *Alte Shul*, southwest entrance.

today Poland's oldest existing synagogue, dating back to the time of King Casimir the Great in the fourteenth century. The *Alte Shul* has been declared a national monument by the *Sejm*, one of only three synagogues in Poland to be given that status, the Nozik synagogue of Warsaw and the Great Synagogue of Wlodowa being the other two.

    The *Alte Shul*, its curators told me, was opened by the government in 1959 as a museum dedicated to Polish-Jewish culture. It had revolving displays of Jewish liturgical artifacts, as well as a photographic exhibit on Nazi Judophobia. During the last few years, however, the museum has been closed to the public, leaving only the chapel open for visitors. The two young curators at the synagogue, both Polish Catholics, were pursuing degrees in Polish-Jewish history at Cracow University; they refused to comment on the closure. They did tell me that the *Alte Shul* had played a prominent role in the national history of Poland. In the course of the various insurrections against foreign domination, patriotic speeches had been given in its sanctuary urging Jews and Poles to unite in defense of their common homeland. Before World War II, the synagogue

3. Cracow. *Alte Shul*, interior. The Gothic *bimah*, with its wrought-iron polygonal grille—a fine example of Polish-Jewish craftsmanship—marked a new trend in synagogue art. The interior design is similar to that of Prague's Old-New Synagogue, with its two naves and ribbed cross-vault supported on two slim pillars. The Holy Ark reflects a late Renaissance influence.

was alleged to be in possession of an ancient manuscript upon which was written a moving prayer for the welfare of King Casimir the Great. The prayer was supposedly read every Sabbath for more than half a millennium.

The Germans began plundering the *Alte Shul* a short time after their entrance into Cracow. They sacked and looted the valuable library and rare manuscripts. The massive bronze chandeliers, a hallmark of the sanctuary, were used to decorate the house of the Nazi Governor General, Hans Frank. The building, used as a warehouse by the Nazis, survived the war with only partial damage.

I was told that, after the war, the edifice remained abandoned and overgrown with vegetation, most of the worshipers having perished in Auschwitz. However, the *Sejm* undertook to restore what it considered at the time a Polish national treasure.

Throughout my conversations with the curators of the *Alte Shul*, it soon became apparent to me that the subject of Polish Jews and Jewish events in Poland were invariably referred to in the past tense, as one would speak, let us say, of an extinct tribe. For them, Polish-Jewish history came to an end in 1945.

A different picture of the closure of the *Alte Shul* museum was presented by a former curator, Dr. Roman Pytel, unemployed since he fell out of favor with the government during the anti-Zionist purges. Speaking in his one-room flat in Cracow, I soon discovered that this closure was linked to politics, since such a museum was too much of an embarrassment for a government indulging in what amounted to anti-Semitic tactics, however disguised.

Pytel was dismissed from his post on charges of Zionism, even though he is a devout Roman Catholic. He holds degrees in Semitics, speaks Hebrew fluently, and spent a year studying in Israel. Dr. Pytel was in the midst of translating into Polish the complete works of the Hebrew Nobel Prize winner, Agnon, having been authorized for the task shortly before the author's death. Pytel's apartment was a clutter of memorabilia:

4. Cracow. Seventeenth-century High Synagogue, now an apartment house.

5. Cracow. Renowned Talmudic Academy on Esther St., abandoned since the war.

an autographed picture of Agnon dedicated to him, menorahs from a fifteenth-century Polish synagogue, rare Hebrew manuscripts, as well as pictures of Kosciuszko and Poland's poet laureate, Adam Mickiewicz. He credited his preoccupation with Judaica as an expression of a desire to return to the "source." He, like many other Polish intellectuals, was giving vent to a form of protest against Soviet domination, with its bogus anti-Zionist campaign, by trying to keep alive the positive aspects of Poland's past glory. And to him, the study of Polish-Jewish history was part and parcel of the national past.

6. Cracow. The sixteenth-century Remo Synagogue, named after one of Judaism's greatest scholars, Rabbi Moses Isserles. It is the only synagogue in the city used on a regular basis.

Leaving the study of the past with Pytel, I set about investigating the present-day situation of Cracow's Jews. At the *Kehilla* (Jewish Communal Headquarters), housed in a building impressive from the outside, but with only two rooms still used by the Jewish community, I was viewed with suspicion by the elderly leaders. They were afraid to comment, other than to say that today only a few hundred Jews lived in the city, which before the war had 75,000. While I was at the *Kehilla*, some bags of soil were being delicately sifted as if for a lost treasure. I was told that the *Kehilla's* major task now was collecting martyrs' bones from

7. Abraham Fogel, cantor of the Remo Synagogue. The Renaissance style of the interior, a single-naved hall with round-headed windows, was similar to that found in Cracow palaces of the period.

8. Cracow. Remo ark. In peculiarly Polish fashion, the *Ner Tamid* (eternal light) was placed in a niche next to the ark, rather than above it, as is the case in most synagogues.

a recently discovered massacre site, for reinterment elsewhere. I was not told where. The only other information I was able to obtain from the *Kehilla* was that Cracow had only one regularly functioning synagogue.

It was on July 4, 1975, that we attended Sabbath services at the historic Remo synagogue, down the square from the *Alte Shul*. The Roman-barrel vaulted edifice, built in the sixteenth century, was named after the famous Talmudic genius, Rabbi Moses Isserles, and had been constructed under the patronage of the Polish King, Sigismund August, in appreciation of the valuable services Cracow Jews were rendering his kingdom.

The square in front of the Remo resembled a picture postcard, with cobblestone streets, lanes weaving like Talmudic arguments, and even an old public well. Seated in the courtyard were several Scholem Aleichem characters, elderly men waiting for the Polish sun to set. There was Abraham Fogel, the *shames* (sexton), who had survived the war as a refugee in Russia, but had lost his entire family in the holocaust. Being the caretaker of this historic synagogue was to him a holy mission, in memory of his martyred family. Then there was Dr. Krug, at 83, the

9. Cracow. Decaying Torah scrolls in the Remo library. They are from the Cracow synagogues that have been closed.

10. Cracow. In Remo courtyard waiting for the sun to set. Facing the camera is Dr. Krug—at 83, the oldest advocate in Cracow.

oldest advocate in Cracow. He, too, managed to survive in Russia, and was now too tired to be uprooted again. Maurice Koszmar served in the Polish cavalry in 1932, and was interned in the Buchenwald concentration camp. That grim experience is borne out by a tattooed number on his arm. Tired old men, waiting for the sun to set on Cracow.

While browsing inside the Remo synagogue, I came across trunks full of Torah scrolls and literally thousands of decaying books. "Take them to America," one old man said, but another quickly added, "The government won't let them out even if they rot in Poland!"

Next to the Remo synagogue, surrounded by high walls, is Poland's oldest existing Jewish cemetery, dating from the sixteenth century. Here lie buried many prominent physicians to Polish kings and Cracow nobility. Miraculously, the only tombstone to survive the war totally unimpaired was that of Rabbi Moses Isserles. Traditionally, on the

11. Maurice Koszmar, a Buchenwald survivor.

12. Cracow. Oldest existing Jewish cemetery in Poland. It was restored with funds from the Joint Distribution Committee of America.

13. Cracow. Tomb of Rabbi Moses Isserles (third from right), the only tombstone in the cemetery to survive the war unimpaired. The epitaph reads: ''From Moses to Moses, there was none like Moses.''

Lag B'omar holiday, Polish Jews came on pilgrimages to Remo's tomb, and even on July 4, 1975, enough of the faithful had survived to have left written supplications around the sage's grave.

A short distance away from the Remo synagogue is the Temple, once the synagogue of Cracow's most prosperous Jews. Even after the devastation by the Nazis, the large, impressive building dominates the neighborhood in its stately elegance. The old *shames* embarrassingly tried to hide from me that he had turned the chapel in the rear into his living quarters. The main sanctuary was still used, he said, on the High Holy Days. Exquisite stained-glass windows and an unusual wrought-iron Ark of the Law were ample evidence of the Temple's prewar splendor and prestige. The grandeur of the building, however, especially from within, gave, in light of the present circumstances, the distinct impression of visiting a mausoleum rather than a house of worship.

14. Cracow. Fading Yiddish sign on pre-war building in the heart of the former Jewish quarter.

15. Dr. Roman Pytel, dismissed from his post as Semitics professor at Cracow University, for alleged ''Zionist'' sentiments. Behind him, on the wall, is a photograph (left) of his teacher who worked on the most recent Polish translation of the Hebrew Bible. To the right is an autographed photograph dedicated to Pytel from Nobel Prize-winning Hebrew author, S. Y. Agnon.

16. Cracow. The Temple, once the synagogue of the city's most prosperous Jews.

17. Cracow. Temple ark, showing wrought-iron gates.

18. Cracow. *Bes Medrash* (House of Study) at 42 Jozefa St. Today, it serves as an apartment house.

19. Cracow. Seventeenth-century *Izaka Shul*, named after Isaac Jakubowicz, the famous banker of King Wladislaw IV. It is now a warehouse.

20. Warsaw. Ghetto Memorial on Anielewicz St. The 36-ft.-high bronze statue portrays Mordecai Anielewicz, the revolt commander, standing in the burning ghetto with his fighters—elderly men, women, and children. The granite of the wall behind had been imported by Hitler for a projected monument to his victory over Polish Jews. On the back of the wall is a bas-relief depicting the contrasting scene of Jews passively going to the slaughter. The inscription at the base of the monument reads in Polish, Hebrew, and Yiddish: "To the Jewish People, its heroes and its martyrs."

21. Warsaw. Mila 18, address of the ghetto uprising headquarters. Today, it designates a new apartment house.

22. Warsaw. Mound at Mila 1, on top of which is a small memorial to the ghetto fighters. New high-rise housing projects cover the former ghetto area in the rubble of which were buried the remains of Warsaw Jewry.

If Cracow is the only city in Poland to have most of its prewar synagogues survive, Warsaw is the only city in Poland today where some form of Jewish prewar communal life survives. The notorious ghetto area, however, which once covered fully one-third of the city, has been totally transformed by new, high-rise apartment buildings, so that nowadays there is no inkling of the area's former role. The massive ghetto monument at the corner of Anielewicz and Zamenhof streets looks out of place amidst the hustle and bustle of the new city. Its thirty-six-foot-high bronze statue of the heroes of the ghetto uprising is the only monument erected by the Polish government to the hundreds of thousands of Jews buried in the rubble upon which rises the new city of Warsaw.

Mila 18, the former headquarters of the Jewish underground, where the ghetto revolt was planned, today is the designation for a new

23. Warsaw. Plaque on former ghetto wall recalling that here was the infamous *Umschlagplatz*, selection center for deportation of Jews to the Treblinka death camp.

apartment house. The underground bunker has been moved to a small park at the beginning of Mila Street, where inscriptions in Polish and Yiddish recall its importance and significance. The only other tribute in the entire former ghetto area, which once housed 600,000 Jews, is a corroding plaque on a factory wall on Stawki Street. In Yiddish it tells that

24. Warsaw. Front view of *Nozik Shul*, only surviving synagogue in city. The building dates from the nineteenth century.

25. Warsaw. Sealed windows of *Nozik Shul*.

this was the location of the infamous *Umschlagplatz*, where the Nazis brutally carried out their selections for deportations to the death camps.

The sole synagogue in Warsaw to survive the war is found in the heart of the prewar Jewish quarter at Plac Grzybowski. Although the government has designated it a national monument as with the *Alte Shul* in Cracow, the building stands with its windows either boarded or bricked up, its brick walls disintegrating, surrounded by neglect and decay. Visitors and worshipers alike were greeted the summer of 1975 by the ominous word *Zyd* (Jew) scribbled across the front doors, reminiscent of a set from a film on the Nazi era. As the door was padlocked, we went next door to the *Kehilla*, which was housed in a large dilapidated, prewar building smelling of neglect. We were greeted by the aroma of soup and the chatter of Yiddish emanating from a public kitchen in which a dozen or so elderly people were sitting. The *mashgiach* (ritual supervisor), a bearded Lubavitch Hasid, welcomed us warmly in fluent Hebrew. He

26. Warsaw. *Nozik Shul*, interior.

27. Warsaw. Lubavitch Hasid, *mashgiach* (ritual supervisor) of *Kehilla*.

alone served the spiritual needs of the *Kehilla* as ritual slaughterer and kosher supervisor, thus holding the dubious honor of being the last Jew in Poland so qualified. He was emphatic about the existence of religious freedom in Poland today, but was quick to add that the forced exodus of Jews left not one rabbi in the entire country, and resulted in the closing of all Jewish schools and youth clubs. "We have become a *Kehilla* without weddings, without *brises* (circumcisions), without *bar mitzvahs*," he sighed, "only funerals." The soup in his public kitchen was plain, but it was kosher.

As we left the *Kehilla*, the Hasid pointed to a plaque on the wall dating the renovation of the building by the chronological age of the modern state of Israel. In light of the anti-Zionist campaign still current, it took on added significance. I asked the Hasid why the Jewish community does not try to keep up and repair the *Kehilla* building. He replied, "Whom should we repair it for? After us there will be no Jews left in Poland."

28. Warsaw. Indigent Jew in *Kehilla* courtyard.

29. Caretaker of Warsaw Jewish cemetery reciting psalms before a funeral.

A different attitude was expressed by the elderly, but still energetic Pinkus, caretaker of Warsaw's huge, historic Jewish cemetery. He thought that the best way to preserve and honor the memory of Polish Jewry was by seeing to it that the institutions built up over the centuries should live on, even if the Jews of Poland disappear. *"Bist du a Yid?"* ("Are you a Jew?") he cautiously greets visitors as they enter the small door in the wall which surrounds the burial ground. A positive response is enough payment for a grand tour through this pantheon of Polish Jewry. Not surprisingly, the cemetery is the busiest center of Warsaw Jews today. Pinkus recalled the role the cemetery played in the smuggling of arms and food into the ghetto during the war, even pointing out the manhole to the sewer that led to the "Aryan" part of Warsaw. The

30. Warsaw. Jewish cemetery.

cemetery bears witness to age and abuse. Vandals, referred to as "hooligans" by Pinkus, continue to desecrate tombs in search of buried "Jewish gold." The government has threatened to raze most of the cemetery for the construction of a highway, a threat taken seriously by Polish Jews, inasmuch as the entire Bialystok cemetery was recently leveled and most of the one in Lublin; there are even rumors of imminent destruction of the great cemetery of Wroclaw, in which are buried Ferdinand Lasalle, founder of the German Socialist movement, and Heinrich Graetz, the celebrated Jewish historian. Most of the Warsaw cemetery, despite the valiant efforts of Pinkus, is an impenetrable overgrowth of trees and bushes, a jungle where roots and vines intertwine with Hebrew letters and epitaphs, where pathways tunnel through what seems to be a forest of the dead.

31. Warsaw. Tomb (center) of Esther Rachel Kaminska, mother of the Warsaw Yiddish Theater.

Buried here is a galaxy of giants of Polish Jewry: Peretz, the famous Yiddish author; Ansky, author of *The Dybbuk*; Dinesohn, the Yiddish novelist; Zamenhof, creator of the international language, Esperanto; Esther Rachel Kaminska, world renowned Yiddish actress; Balaban, the historian—to name but a few of the hundreds of authors, artists, rabbis, scholars, and other notables who rest so precariously in this hall of fame.

32. Warsaw. A literary pantheon. Buried here are I. L. Peretz (1851-1915), Yiddish writer; Jacob Dinesohn (1858-1919), Yiddish novelist; and S. Ansky (1863-1920), author.

33. Warsaw. Bas-relief on the tomb of Dov Baer Shmulovicz, a member of nineteenth-century Poland's most prominent commercial family and ancestor of Henri Bergson, the Nobel Prize-winning French philosopher. Cargo ships symbolize the deceased's fame in foreign trade, while the harps and willows are symbols of mourning based upon Psalm 137. A castle adjacent to a synagogue depicts the close relationship of the family with Poland's kings. The family once was immortalized in Polish folklore for its crucial role in Poland's economic development; today its name has been removed from all school texts, and its mausoleum vandalized many times over.

34. Warsaw. Tomb of the Landau family.

35. Warsaw. A wall made from vandalized tombstones.

36. Warsaw. Recently vandalized tomb of a surgeon, Dr. Szanger.

37. Warsaw. A Treblinka survivor tends family grave.

38. Warsaw. Forest of the dead.

39. Warsaw. Manhole to sewer, once the key lifeline of the ghetto, where food and arms were smuggled in from the "Aryan" side.

Pinkus claims that the upkeep of the cemetery relies heavily upon donations from America, which have been few and far between these last few years. Yet Pinkus continues his battle against the encroachments of nature, against vandalism, against governmental indifference, but most of all for the memory of a thousand-year-old civilization whose heroes lie buried here.

40. Lodz. Scenes at Jewish People's Club, the last such club in the entire Lodz province.

41. Lodz. Interior of the only synagogue left in the city. It is a small, rather modern structure, hidden away in a courtyard.

42. Lodz. Jozef Poznanski mausoleum in the Jewish cemetery. Poznanski was a twentieth-century textile magnate. Polish-Jewish funerary art, of which the Lodz cemetery offers the finest examples, developed over the centuries a complex system of symbols reflective of those values and virtues which Polish Jews considered of importance to memorialize on their tombs, such as scholarship, philanthropy, and ancestry. Books or a Torah crown meant scholarship; an alms box, charity; running water or musical instruments, Levite ancestry. Cut trees symbolized an early death; leafless branches, parents without children. Various animals indicated the name of the deceased: e.g., a deer (Hirsch), a dove (Jonah), a stag (Zev), a sheep (Rebecca), a fish (Fischel).

43. Lodz. The caretaker of the cemetery.

44. Lodz. Intricately carved sarcophagus of a Lodz surgeon, Dr. Silberstern (1876-1907).

45. Lodz. Cows feeding over a scholar's tomb. The hands on the tombstone indicate that the deceased was a *cohen*, member of the priestly tribe, while the Torah crown symbolizes scholarship.

Pinkus has a counterpart in only one other city in Poland, and that is in Lodz, which before the war had 250,000 Jews. Here the task of caring for the vast cemetery lies on the shoulders of a Jewish dwarf. As in Warsaw, in Lodz the Jewish cemetery is enormous, historic, and totally overgrown with thirty years of uncontrolled vegetation. The available funds for its upkeep are even more limited than in Warsaw, since fewer tourists go there and fewer people outside of Poland know of its existence. Some of the most beautiful examples of Jewish funerary art in the world, however, are found in the Lodz cemetery. Magnificent sarcophagi and mausoleums of mammoth size and fascinating shapes abound there, erected to commemorate the textile magnates who established the city's vast industrial complex. Most of the cemetery, surprisingly enough, survived the war intact, even though the entire Baluty ghetto area bordering it was leveled.

46. Wegrow. The recently bulldozed cemetery, converted by the municipality into a soccer field.

Like Pinkus in Warsaw, Moshe Lekken in Lodz sees himself as the last curator of an extinct civilization. "When I go, so will this cemetery," he lamented. Behind him cows were grazing over the tombs of saintly sages.

The fate of countless other Jewish burial grounds throughout Poland, without a Pinkus or a Moshe to look after them, is another tragic chapter in these last days of Polish Jewry. In Wegrow, the townspeople were ashamed to tell us where the Jewish cemetery was; some even denied there ever was one, despite the fact that the town had been fifty percent Jewish before the war. It was a small boy who led us to a new soccer field, at the end of which were piled like a heap of refuse the broken tombs of the Jews who stayed behind in Wegrow. Rare were the towns like Lukow, where the memory of its Jews was preserved by a monument made from the scattered, broken tombs of the cemetery. Most villages have turned them into grazing fields for the cows or, at worst, garbage dumps. In Krasnik, Jewish tombs were used to pave a side street, the Hebrew epitaphs still clearly visible.

47. Lukow. The tombstone monument erected by death-camp survivors following the war. No Jews remain in the village, which was 50 percent Jewish in 1939.

48. Scholars at Warsaw's Jewish Historical Institute.

Leaving the Warsaw cemetery behind, we headed for the Jewish Historical Institute housed in what was once a wing of Warsaw's Great Synagogue at Plac Tlomacki. It is a state-supported institution founded in 1945 as part of the Polish Academy of Science, and has one of the most outstanding collections of Judaica in the world (60,000 volumes). The collection was assembled from the remnants of Jewish libraries and museums all over Poland. Among its rare items, none of which are allowed out of Poland on exhibit, are a ninth-century manuscript of the legendary Jewish traveler, Eldad Ha-Dani, letters of Spinoza's teacher, medieval prayer books, and Bibles. Also in the Institute's possession is a vast collection of paintings by Polish-Jewish artists, liturgical artifacts of every variety, and the complete archives of Emmanuel Ringelblum, whose diary was found after the war in sealed cans, and is today considered the most complete record of the daily unfolding of the Warsaw Ghetto tragedy. All these items, and many more, are displayed for public viewing in a museum which is located on the top two floors of the building, which also houses an extensive exhibit on the holocaust.

Drastically diminished by the exodus of Polish Jews in 1968, the Institute staff is now composed of only a few Jewish scholars. They still manage, however, to publish a scholarly bulletin dealing with topics varying from the scientific research carried out at the Warsaw Jewish Hospital before the war by two famed neurologists, to the rise of the great Jewish labor unions in Bialystok; from eyewitness accounts of Nazi atrocities, to a detailed analysis of Polish synagogue architecture.

"Due to the political climate, our bulletin must now appear in Polish and not Yiddish," lamented one of the Institute scholars. "Hardly anyone, therefore, outside of Poland is able to read it, and hardly anyone in Poland wants to."

The Institute staff has been subjected to strict governmental surveillance, and its contacts with foreigners are often restricted. A former staff member told me that an atmosphere of apprehension and even fear pervades the place. There have been threats to close the museum, and even to end the scholarly research.

This former employee of the Institute, who insisted that his name be withheld, recalled in lurid detail the harassment of Polish Jews following the 1968 riots, how people had been dismissed from government posts and university positions merely for having a Jewish grandparent, of how totally assimilated Jews who had absolutely no contact with the Jewish community, overnight found themselves jobless and ostracized by their neighbors.

A special department of the Ministry of the Interior, employing one hundred people and headed by a Colonel Tadeusz Walichnowski, had been set up to investigate Jewish ancestry among government officials, the family trees being kept on reference for "security reasons."

A group of Jewish students, whose fathers had been in the government service, were put on trial in 1968 as Zionists who had actively rejected Golmulka's return to power in 1956. The fact that none of the accused was more than seven years old in 1956 was not seen by the inquisitors as convincing enough evidence of the innocence of the accused.

An extremely popular television show called "Questions and Answers" devoted a series to exposing Zionism, replete with illustrations of long-nosed hunchbacks wearing the star of David. Zionists were linked to everything from high meat prices to student riots, from the scarcity of women's nylons to electric power failures.

A Jewish couple was put on public trial for having influenced their son, who supposedly was a leader of the riots. It was only much later reported that the couple had been childless.

A lawyer with a Jewish-sounding surname was arrested as a Zionist, and acquitted only after he had proven that he was a descendant of a well-known Catholic family.

Zionist students were blamed for the riots at several major universities where not one Jewish student was in attendance.

All this, unfolding in a land where the Nazi crematoria had not even had time to cool . . . Jews again had to walk the streets of Poland in fear and trepidation, cautiously restrained from speaking Yiddish in public for fear of accusations of conspiring in a foreign tongue, hesitant about entering a synagogue, apprehensive about their precarious livelihood, pessimistic about their future. Those who were not too old or too ill to emigrate during that period, did so; those few who remained waited out the storm with the silent stoicism of a people schooled in suffering.

The informant had mixed feelings about the reaction of the Catholic Church to these outbursts of government-sponsored anti-Semitism in the guise of anti-Zionism. On the one hand, some church leaders who were strongly opposed to the atheistic regime openly voiced their indignation. A few churches even dared to show films on Israel at the height of the anti-Zionist outbreak. A group of over one hundred Catholic youths from a major Warsaw church spent several weeks during their school vacation doing volunteer work in the Warsaw cemetery, helping the *Kehilla* in its efforts at restoration. A Warsaw priest inaugurated an annual tradition of saying a special Mass for the Jewish victims of Nazism, and even carried on a one-man crusade to have Janusz Korczak declared a national saint. Korczak, a renowned Polish-Jewish author, pedagogue, and social worker, had voluntarily gone to his death during World War II in order to accompany the little children of his orphanage to the gas chambers.

On the other hand, Poland's Cardinal Hlond did not publicly alter his stand, held since 1936, of accusing Jews of sponsoring atheism and Bolshevism in Poland. Thus, the church hierarchy remained deafeningly silent during this period, as it had during the Nazi holocaust.

The only Jews found in Poland today who are able to speak openly to foreigners without fear of repercussions are the editors of *Folks-sztyme* (Peoples' Voice), the last Yiddish newspaper in Poland. Prior to World War II, Poland had twenty-seven Yiddish dailies and one hundred weeklies. The greatest Yiddish newspaper in the world, *Haint* (Today) was published in Warsaw. It had over one thousand correspondents and was read by millions of Jews throughout the world. Among its contributors had been David Ben Gurion and Shalom Asch. *Haint* came out twice daily, with a special weekend supplement every Friday. This newspaper organized contests with sets of Talmuds and Bibles as prizes. It even sponsored trips to Palestine in which as many as eight hundred people participated. The last issue appeared on September 22, 1939, and contained selections from the Psalms as its requiem.

In the early 1950's, *Folks-sztyme* made a concerted effort to inform its readers honestly in the great *Haint* tradition, even going so far as to criticize the Soviet Union for being the main source of contemporary anti-Semitism. Today, however, it is totally a mouthpiece of the Polish Communist Party and has been turned into a weekly publication.

Samuel Tenenblat, the relatively young editor, talked openly and candidly in his new, wood-paneled office. A committed member of the Polish Communist Party, he had graduated with a degree in Marxism from Warsaw University. The ideology of the paper was thus admittedly Marxist, but, he was quick to add, proudly Yiddishist as well.

Before the war, Poland had a small, but growing, minority of Yiddish secularists, mainly in the urban areas. Representing an entire spectrum of political ideologies, they expressed their Jewishness linguistically, rather than religiously. They ran their own Yiddish institutions—

49. Editors of *Folks-sztyme*, Poland's last Yiddish newspaper.

schools, scout groups, cooperatives (over 500), newspapers, and were represented in the Polish parliament along with the religious bloc. In the rural areas, such Yiddish secularists were often branded as *apikorsim* (atheists) for their unpardonable sin of shaving their beards, or, even worse, appearing in public bare-headed. Tenenblat is among the last of this breed. He gloried in Yiddish culture, but only as a medium for socialist ends.

Tenenblat was admittedly concerned by the synagogue and cemetery desecrations and other kinds of vandalism, but attributed it to misguided hooligans. As for the recent purges which had destroyed the lives of so many of his fellow Jewish Marxists, causing their exodus from Poland, he had no comment other than to strike back with "and there is no anti-Semitism in your America?"

Before the most recent purges, a few Jewish secularists had risen in the Polish bureaucratic hierarchy to important posts, including a vice premier, an ambassador to London, three Supreme Court justices, and several prominent professors, attorneys, and physicians. Tenenblat was well aware that not one of these now remained in Poland, but was still unwilling to connect this to anti-Semitism. He reluctantly agreed that he would probably be the last editor of Poland's last Yiddish newspaper. A clear indication, at any rate, was the fact that Samuel Tenenblat, one of the few "young" Jews left in Poland, had married a non-Jew and none of his children spoke a word of Yiddish.

Next door to the *Folks-sztyme* office at Plac Grzybowski, and in stark contrast to the run-down synagogue and dilapidated *Kehilla*, is the ultramodern building of the Yiddish State Theater. In 1939, Warsaw boasted of six full-time Yiddish theaters, and one hundred other Jewish troupes were active throughout the country.

The present theater building was opened in 1970 at the cost of $1,250,000 and is totally subsidized by the government. Its founder and star performer, Ida Kaminska, fled Poland in 1968, yet the show goes on three times a week.

50. Scene from
a production at the
Yiddish State
Theater.

51. Warsaw.
Street posters
announcing
plays at the
Yiddish State
Theater.

It was Ida's mother, Esther Rachel Kaminska (1868-1925), who introduced to Yiddish repertoire the European classics of Shakespeare, Chekhov, and Shaw, and Ida had carried on her mother's tradition. Under Ida Kaminska, the Warsaw Yiddish theater had maintained a world-wide reputation. Now, in 1975, the theater has an ironic aspect of tragicomedy. Earphones are provided to give simultaneous translations for the now almost exclusively Polish audiences. Since there are no longer any Jewish actors or actresses in Poland other than the handful still associated with the Warsaw theater, the government has had to train young Polish theater students to speak Yiddish. Productions have had to incorporate more music and cut out much Yiddish dialogue. The net result is that rabbinical characters in Yiddish plays end up being played by Catholics speaking a broken Yiddish with a pronounced Polish accent. Hence the strange anomaly that the only "rabbis" left in Poland—are Catholic!

Why does the Polish government continue to subsidize such a charade? Aside from the obvious propaganda value of having a Yiddish theater in the nation's capital, where hundreds of thousands of foreign tourists come annually, there seems to be a genuine interest in the productions among many Poles. At least, that is what several Jewish residents of Warsaw claim, and quite a few Poles do attend the plays throughout the year. This interest, I was told, is a result of "nostalgia" and curiosity. "The negative publicity given to Zionism has had a reverse reaction among intellectuals, especially the youth," one Jewish theatergoer observed. "There is a skepticism about everything the government says, even if it is about Jews. Thus, people come here out of a general inquisitiveness."

What the audience sees, however, is hardly an accurate picture of the Jewish past in Poland—probably the main reason why the government allows the theater to continue. The repertoire consists of carefully selected prewar Yiddish plays, totally innocuous and highly romanticized. The scenarios portray quaint caricatures of gesticulating Jews, who spend their time in exotic dance and song, spouting comic witticisms or mystical incantations; Jews whose only "tragic" moments involve trying to find suitable marriage partners for their children, or exorcizing *dybbuks* (evil spirits) from possessed women.

"It's as if these works of fiction have taken the place of history," grieved one Warsaw Jew. "Young people leave the theater with the impression that prewar Jewish life in Poland actually was as it is portrayed on the stage—as if all the horrors of anti-Semitic prejudice and violence never existed here except under the Nazis."

With this theater's increasingly becoming the only place in Poland to view anything remotely resembling Jewish life, the real tragedy is that future generations of Poles will, indeed, know "Jews" only as caricatures with a two-hour life span on the stage of Warsaw's last Yiddish theater.

Leaving Warsaw and the other major cities, we decided to head into Galicia, the heartland of prewar Jewish life. We were especially anxious to see if any of the famous four-pillared synagogues had survived the holocaust and what had become of those that did. For only in Poland had the Jews in the Diaspora succeeded in creating an independent architectural style. This had been a result of two major factors: their long period of permanent settlement in Poland, compared to the constant expulsions and movements elsewhere in the world, and the unique nature of the liturgical emphasis among Eastern European Jews.

The oldest synagogue structure in Poland, the *Alte Shul* of Cracow, had been architecturally a copy of the medieval synagogue style found throughout Europe. It was a double-naved, two pillared edifice, with the *bimah* (the Torah reader's platform) slightly elevated between the two columns.

A disparity soon arose, however, between this inherited motif and the Polish liturgical emphasis which placed the reading of the Torah as the central and most important act of worship. The conflict was resolved in the sixteenth century with the creation of the centrally-located, four-columned *bimah* which, covered with a canopy, supported the ceiling by connecting to the roof in four sweeping ribs, with four lofty barrel vaults. This served as the sole means of support for the entire roof of the hall of prayer, thus enabling all worshipers around the *bimah* to have an unobstructed view of the Torah reading, as well as providing the best in acoustics.

Thus, the four-pillared synagogue not only solved the problem of a centrally conceived liturgical function, but historically is a major Jewish contribution to religious architecture.

Of special interest is the fact that these stone synagogues were constructed partly underground, so that the main hall of worship was often many feet below street level. Later in history, pious Jews sought to explain this as in keeping with Psalm 130.1, "Out of the depths have I called thee, O Lord!" Historians, however, see it as an attempt to circumvent the Polish church law which forbade synagogue buildings to rise above a certain prescribed height. By sinking the synagogue below street level, an inner spaciousness was created without violating the external restrictions.

It was in Poland, also, that synagogue polychromy, wood carving, and hammered brass and copper took on a unique character and style. For, unlike Jews in other countries, the Jews of Poland, rather than hired non-Jews, were the artisans and painters, the carpenters and coppersmiths who decorated their houses of worship, thus imparting their own characteristic peculiarities and artistic expression.

Synagogue polychromy in Poland reached its peak in the seventeenth century, with motifs reflective of the pastoral environment in which the Polish Jews lived. Inspiration was drawn not only from Biblical and Talmudic themes, but also from Polish peasant folklore. The proscription against human images led to the development of a complex and intricate system of symbols.

It was in the medium of wood, however, that Polish Jews attained their greatest artistic achievements. In a land where timber is plentiful, they constructed vast pagoda-like wooden synagogues. Some were topped with cupolas to give a tent-like effect. Others had entrance porches built in the form of classical porticoes. The interiors were phantasmogorias of Biblical beasts, flora and fauna, zodiacal signs, and inscriptions from sacred texts, frequently covering all available space on the walls, as well as ceilings. So impressive were these wooden synagogues that the prewar Polish government allocated funds for their restoration and preservation. Ironically, German museums prior to the Nazis, were eager to acquire such Polish synagogue carvings and ornamentation as precious works of art.

The search for surviving examples of this unique synagogue art and architecture took us to many remote villages in Poland. In Zamosc,

52. Zamosc. Classical fortress-type synagogue. Built in 1610, the roof is equipped with a fortified parapet and shooting loopholes. The building now serves as the town library.

the birthplace of the Yiddish writer Isaac Leib Peretz, we found that the town's fortress-type synagogue had survived the war intact. It remains as one of the most outstanding archetypes of late Renaissance Jewish sacral style. Built in 1610, in an era when this area of Poland was often beseiged by Cossacks, it was designed partly for defense purposes, its roof surrounded by a fortified parapet equipped with shooting loopholes and crenellated cornices. The interior, with its square monastic vaulting, had been especially renowned for its polychrome frescoes and ornamental stucco. These reflected an Italian influence, as Zamosc was situated on a major trade route with Italy. While the building has survived the ravages of both the Cossacks and, later in history, the Nazis, the frescoes fell victim to the post-war Zamosc authorities, who in confiscating the edifice for use as the town library, wantonly painted over the interior with whitewash.

53. Rzeszow. The massive, seventeenth-century Nowomiejska (New Town) Synagogue. It is now a museum of Polish art. The upper story was added in 1965. The entrance is below street level.

In Rzeszow, a Galician town once forty percent Jewish, but where today not a single Jew is to be found, two huge four-pillared synagogues remain. The town officials have converted the structures–one into a museum of Polish art, the other into the municipal archives. In Rzeszow, unlike in most other Polish towns where surviving synagogues have been appropriated for different use, the municipality has placed plaques on the buildings recalling their former role. The one at the entrance to the museum states: "The Nowomiejska Synagogue, built in the XVII century, vandalized by the Nazi barbarians in 1944. It was restored in 1965 for the advancement and popularization of art in our province."

While in the city of Tarnow, which was forty-five percent Jewish before the war, and like most other towns in Poland today, is now *Judenrein*, we found an interesting park on ul. Zydowska ("Jewish Street"). In the middle of the park, whose entrance gates bear stars of David, stands a stone four-pillared *bimah*. It is, I later discovered, the sole remnant of a great fortress-type synagogue which was constructed in 1582 and stood on the grounds of the present park. The municipality kept it there on display as a work of art, but without any explanation as to what it was.

In the town of Lancut, the director of Orbis (the official Polish travel bureau) proved extremely helpful in taking us to the town's

54. Tarnow park, former site of the town's Great Synagogue. Note the four-pillared *bimah* inside.

55. Lancut. The eighteenth-century synagogue, the exterior of which was recently renovated by the municipality.

four-pillared synagogue, constructed in 1750 in Baroque style. The city had spent the equivalent of $100,000 on its renovation, but was still undecided as to its future function. The interior once was so renowned for its rococo polychrome murals, that Stanislaw August Poniatowski, the last king of Poland, crowned in 1764, commissioned the artist Zygmunt Vogel to reproduce them in watercolor. It seems that the Lancut synagogue originally had been built under the patronage of the local count Lubomirski. In his exquisite castle, now a public museum, we chanced upon a seven-foot menorah inscribed in Polish, stating that it was presented to the count by the Lancut Jewish community on the occasion of his daughter's marriage.

The last place in which we found an example of the four-pillared synagogue was in the Galician town of Rymanow, the former seat of the Hasidic Rymanower Rebbe. Built in the sixteenth century as the most prominent structure in the entire area, it is now an empty hulk, with weeds covering its roof. Even though exposed to the elements for thirty-three years, the precious polychrome murals in the interior still retain their former glory.

56. Lancut. Synagogue, interior. A classic example of Polish synagogue architecture. The four pillars carry an arcuated square block of masonry which covers the *bimah* like a canopy. On the block rest four barrel-vaults which rise from the four outer walls of the sanctuary, intersect at the corners, and form a continuous vaulted space around the ark. The superstructure of the *bimah* is decorated with symbolic deer carrying the crown of the Torah. This motif and that of the polychrome murals is from the popular Mishnaic theme (*Ethics of the Fathers*, V, 23) found in Polish synagogues. The cartouches in the stucco decoration are in rococo style.

57. Rymanow. The Great Synagogue. A superb example of
the unique, four-pillared fortress synagogue of Poland.

58. The director of the Lancut Orbis (left) discusses the
uncertain future of the synagogue with the town's doctor,
who is also an expert on Lancut history.

59. Menorah in Lancut castle, now a museum.

60. Rymanow. The Great Synagogue, interior, showing the centrally located four-pillared *bimah*. The magnificent polychrome murals, though exposed to the elements for 33 years, still retain their majesty. The mural on the left depicts the artist's conception of the Wailing Wall in Jerusalem; the other murals are of animals, based upon a Mishnaic teaching, popular among Polish Jews: "Be strong as a leopard, light as an eagle, fleet as a deer, and bold as a lion, to do the will of thy Father in Heaven" (*Ethics of the Fathers*, V, 23).

Surprisingly enough, many synagogues in Poland survived the holocaust. The town of Lesko, which before the war was sixty percent Jewish, restored its huge sixteenth-century synagogue, even keeping the Hebrew ten commandments on its roof, while converting its interior into a museum of Polish art. The city hired a Cracow professor to do a detailed historical analysis of the edifice, and distributes free copies of his findings to visitors.

61. Lesko. The sixteenth-century Great Synagogue, now a museum of Polish art.

A few miles across the rolling Galician countryside from Lesko, however, many residents of the village of Sanok, including the Orbis director, were emphatic in insisting that Sanok had never had a synagogue. This seemed most unusual since Jews had lived there for more than six hundred years, having formed forty-five percent of the prewar population. After receiving only negative, sometimes hostile, responses to my question *"Czy pan pamieta gdzie byta synagoga?"* ("Do you remember where the synagogue was?"), we finally were escorted into a ghetto-like courtyard by an elderly Polish man, who pointing to a rather large structure, sighed *"boznica"* ("God's House," a Polish term for synagogue). In spite of a sign stating *Dom Handlowy* (commercial building), the man's claim was corroborated by the architectural style of the building, and more importantly, a *mezzuzah* hole in the doorpost. For in the process of Polonizing so much of confiscated Jewish property during and after the war, many a *mezzuzah*, which every pious Jew places on or in his doorpost, was overlooked. There they remain to this day, silent witnesses to a truth that some Polish towns, like Sanok, would prefer to forget.

62. Lesko. The Jewish cemetery, where excellent examples of Renaissance funerary art can be found. The synagogue can be seen above the trees.

63. Piotrkow-Trybunalski.
The municipal library,
formerly the town's
Great Synagogue.

64. Przemysl.
The Moshe Sheinbach Synagogue.
Closed by the Nazis in 1939,
it houses today the town library.

65. Polish librarian in former Sheinbach chapel reminisces about prewar days.

A curious case is Piotrkow-Trybunalski, south of Lodz, where on the one hand the town restored its Great Synagogue, converting it into a Polish library, even keeping the two stars of David on the front of the building. At the same time, however, in the interior, an eighteenth-century polychrome mural of the ten commandments is kept hidden behind curtains. I chanced upon it purely by accident, and the head librarian was adamant in her refusal to allow us to photograph it. For some reason the town of Piotrkow is embarrassed by this mural of the tablets of the Law; yet at the same time it refrains from painting it over, as has been done to so much of synagogue polychromy in the rest of Poland.

In the city of Przemysl, the enormous Moshe Sheinbach synagogue has also been converted into a library; today it houses, among other things, an original musical score of Chopin. Przemysl is one of the rare small cities in Poland today where a few Jews are left—twenty-seven to be exact. When one elderly Jew was asked how he felt about the Great Synagogue being converted into the town library, he retorted, "Thank God, they made it into something worthy of the great edifice. In West Przemysl, the synagogue was transformed into a garage!"

66. "Who will say *kaddish* for us?" cries one of the last Jews of Przemysl.

The major concern of the Jews of Przemysl, like that of many other elderly Jews isolated and lonely in small towns of Poland, was not so much the fate of their beloved synagogues, as what would become of their bodies after their death. "Who will be left here to say *kaddish* for us?" they sighed.

67. Przemysl. The former Jewish Hospital.

In Gorlice, the town commemorated their martyred Jews by a small plaque on a wall of the town bakery, seemingly an odd place for such a memorial. On inquiry, however, we were told that it had been the local synagogue. The bakery's supervisor, who is also the regional chairman of the Communist Party, beamed with pride to be able to show off the achievements of socialism to Western tourists. His bakery, we were told, was able to produce enough bread for the entire Gorlice area. Inside, pointing to what to us was obviously the woman's gallery before the metamorphosis, I asked if that was where the pious Jewish women of Gorlice once prayed. "Women? Prayer?" he laughed, "You mean the grain storage area." This time I pointed to where the Ark of the Law must have stood. He instantly responded, "The automatic sifter." Finally, I pointed to what appeared to be the location of the memorial tablets where generations of Gorlice Jews must once have been listed. "The charts of our production quotas," he boasted. And so it was that in Gorlice, Communist technology was able to transform centuries of Jewish life into the most efficient bakery in the province.

68. Przemysl. Ghetto portal,
all that remains of the vast area
which once housed 20,000 Jews.

69. Wlodawa. The seventeenth-
century Great Synagogue. Since
the deportation of this
Jewish community (70 percent
of the town) to Sobibor
death camp in 1942, the synagogue
has been used as a
municipal garage.

70. Wlodawa. Southern view
of the Great Synagogue, one
of the finest examples of Polish-
Jewish architecture.

In the unlikely place of Wlodawa, on the Soviet border, is to be found in Poland the last example of an eighteenth-century style in synagogue art, commemorating the musical instruments of the Temple in Jerusalem with polychrome murals and wood carvings of drums, trumpets, fifes, and violins. In Wlodawa, the government's concern for Jewish art seemed not attributable to ulterior motives, since tourists seldom, if ever, ventured into this forgotten province. It was a tedious journey through what seemed like endless countryside. One could, however, sense the close proximity of the border by the growing size of the Red Army monuments in the town squares.

The Great Synagogue of Wlodawa was not difficult to find, because it was conspicuously situated and, surprisingly, served as the garage of the town's cooperative. Many chapels surrounded the main sanctuary compound. Only the main hall of worship, however, was being restored, scaffolding covering its intricately carved, wooden Baroque ark. The central building dated from the early seventeenth century; the others reflected later additions.

Many of the once lovely chapels are filled with spare parts for automobiles, and above a small ark in one of the chapels the fading Hebrew inscription still proclaims "Know before whom thou stands."

Some workers took us to a tunnel under the main sanctuary ark, which they had discovered in the process of restoration. "This is where the Jews had hidden their gold," they told us, and in many ways it proved to be true, for this had been one of those places found in every synagogue, where Jews buried their most valuable treasures—prayer books and Bibles which had worn out after centuries of continual use. There they remained to that day, the buried "gold" of the Jews of Wlodawa.

71. The Baroque ark of Wlodowa, showing Biblical *shofar* with contemporary violin. The ark, which is undergoing restoration, remains the only example left in the world of an eighteenth-century motif in synagogue art.

72. Wroclaw. The nineteenth-century Storch Synagogue within the former Breslau Jewish Theological Seminary, cradle of Reform and Conservative Judaism. The building was vandalized following the 1967 Israel-Arab war.

One of the most important synagogues to survive the holocaust in Poland is notable not for its art or architecture, but for the fact that it is in an important sense the birthplace of American Judaism. Located in the town of Wroclaw, the major city in Lower Silesia, near the East German border, the Storch synagogue was spared destruction only because it had been sheltered by adjacent buildings. Erected in 1829, it was the largest synagogue in this formerly Germanized city.

The building complex which had surrounded it before the war was the Breslau (German name for Wroclaw) Jewish Theological Seminary, the first modern school for the training of rabbis, which later became the model for rabbinical schools throughout the world. Its faculty included the leaders of the reform movement in Judaism, as well as the founder of what today in America is called Conservative Judaism, Zachariah Frankel.

73. Wroclaw-Storch Synagogue. Interior showing desecrated ark. The two women's galleries, surrounded by a wrought-iron latticed grille, are a unique feature.

Between 1854 and 1938, 250 rabbis were ordained here. The last ordination took place clandestinely on February 21, 1939. During the holocaust, most students and professors were sent to the death camps, and the celebrated library of 30,000 volumes and 400 rare manuscripts was packed into a freight train for shipment to Germany. After the war, the unopened boxcars were found with many of the books intact. They were subsequently shipped to Warsaw, where today they are housed at the Jewish Historical Institute.

The Seminary did not reopen after the war, but instead was converted into the local *Kehilla*, housing a soup kitchen, Hebrew school, administrative offices, an ORT* workshop, and apartments for elderly and indigent Jews.

---

*Organization for Rehabilitation and Training, a Jewish Social Service Agency.

74. Wroclaw. Shoes of Nazi victims in Storch Synagogue.

75. Wroclaw. Room in Seminary compound used as a synagogue by Wroclaw Jews.

76. Wroclaw. Auschwitz survivors.

In the summer of 1975, the Hebrew and ORT schools were no longer functioning, although the administrative offices operated with a skeleton crew. The soup kitchen continues to function, and within the complex still live most of the few remaining Jews of Wroclaw, elderly refugees who were repatriated from the Soviet Union after the war.

As for the Storch synagogue, it stands empty, windows smashed, doors boarded up; a victim not of the Nazis, but of Poland's anti-Zionist vandalism of 1967. The government has confiscated the building and the fate of this cradle of American Judaism remains unknown.

In the congested industrial and coal basin of Upper Silesia, once the home of tens of thousands of Jews, and where, following World War II, a major effort had been made to restore Jewish life, not a single synagogue building survived the holocaust. Today, the few Jews scattered in the vast metropolitan regions of Upper Silesia–in Katowice, Gliwice, Bytom and Sosnowiec—use several small apartments for worship.

Of the numerous Yiddish culture clubs established in Silesia after the war by Jews repatriated from the Soviet Union, only the one in Gliwice still exists, but, ironically, in name only. It is well known in the town as *Klub Zydowski* (The Jewish Club), has a display case of Marxist literature in Yiddish in the lobby, and is tastefully decorated with paintings on Jewish cultural themes. What makes *Klub Zydowski* unique, however, is that since 1969, nearly all of its members are Poles, who come in the evenings to play cards and watch television. An elderly Jewish member, one of the very few, ushered us into a wing of the club no longer in use. Here was located an extensive but dusty Yiddish library and a collection of yellowing photographs of the club's past activities, including one of a Hannukah party held as recently as 1968, before the last major exodus of Polish Jews. Judging from the age of the few Jews who belong, there is little doubt that *Klub Zydowski* in Gliwice will eventually be the only club in the world referred to as Jewish, without having any Jewish members at all.

In Bedzin, north of Katowice, a town once fifty percent Jewish, where Jews had developed the enormous nonferrous metal foundries, the historic Jewish quarter surrounding a fourteenth-century castle built by Casimir the Great lies in ruins, partially hidden under thick vegetation.

Only in Kalisz, north of Upper Silesia, where Jews had been among the founders of the town in the twelfth century and where they had formed fifty percent of the pre-holocaust population, has something of the historic Jewish past survived in this entire region. Here is to be found a curious wall, but not of a synagogue. The wall, the last remnant of a castle built by Casimir the Great, has been the focal point of an unusual story, according to which Casimir had a secret Jewish mistress, Esther, referred to by the endearing Polish form of Esterka. She supposedly bore him two sons, who were raised as Catholics and went on to found two of Poland's most illustrious noble families. In Kalisz today, people refer to the wall as the Esterka wall, since it in there that the romantic

77. Rabka. Former synagogue (left), Hebrew school, and rabbi's home (right) in a remote village.

episode was supposed to have transpired. This legend of Esther has found its way into much of Polish folk literature in a variety of forms, including one account in which Esther's ghost is haunting the wall each night in search of her royal lover. Be that as it may, the sad fact remains that other than the spirit of Esther, no Jews nor any remnant of their centuries-old civilization are to be found in this ancient region north of Silesia.

We encountered the same sad facts again and again: In Jozefow, the synagogue is now a wheat silo; in Dukla, a market; in Turek, a cooperative; in Kutno, birthplace of the famed Yiddish author, Shalom Asch, the synagogue stands on Asch St., but now is an office; in Jaslo, a restaurant. In Rabka, once a popular Jewish summer resort in the Tatra Mountains, the synagogue and adjacent Hebrew school are now private houses, while the many formerly Jewish hotels are still functioning, with kosher cooking and the Yiddish language conspicuously absent. In Bochnia, near Cracow, the synagogue is now a warehouse, yet the statue of King Casimir the Great, erected in bygone days by the Jewish community in his honor, still stands in the town square. The relief at the base that explained this fact, however, has been eradicated.

78. Jaroslaw. Interior of the Great Synagogue, constructed in 1805. Located at Plac Boznica (Synagogue Square), it now serves as an art school.

79. Jaroslaw. The pre-war Yiddish Theater, now a Polish culture house.

In Ostroleka, the synagogue is now a garage; in Jaroslaw, an art school; in Radymno, a factory; in Pinczow, a museum; in Strzyzow, a library; in Debica and Chrzanow, a warehouse. In Bialystok, once nearly half Jewish, and where Jews built the vast textile industry, not one Jew nor synagogue is to be found, and the vast cemetery has recently been razed by the Polish government. In Chelm, celebrated in Jewish folklore as the habitat of simpletons, the synagogue is now a technological school; while the Great Synagogue of Czestochowa has become a symphony hall, and the large Jewish hospital, one of fifty that existed in prewar Poland, has been appropriated by the municipality and unceremoniously renamed. In Konin, birthplace of Michael Goldwasser, grandfather of Barry Goldwater, the once magnificent synagogue renowned for its frescoes, stands abandoned; as does the huge synagogue of Nowy Sacz in the Carpathian Mountains, those of Krasnik, south of Lublin, Leczna, near Lodz, and Szydlowiec, which was eighty percent Jewish before the war. Of all the precious wooden synagogues, once considered national treasures of Poland, not one was spared the fires of the holocaust. And so the sad story is repeated, on and on, in town after town, where the pious prayers of centuries have been forever silenced.

80. Chelm. The former synagogue, now a school of technology.

81. Chelm. The only tomb left standing in the historic Jewish cemetery.

82. Czestochowa. The former Jewish Hospital.

Prayer had not been the only pillar of Polish Jewry; study and scholarship were equally important. Even in the poorest of homes could be found a well-used library, and into the late hours of the night bent many, laboring over the holy books after a hard day's work. To be poor was no blessing to Polish Jews, but to be an *am-haaretz* (ignoramus) was to be truly cursed. It was thus no accident that in Poland had been located many, if not most, of the greatest world centers of Talmudic study, the yeshivas; and nowhere else in the world had there been a yeshiva like that of *Yeshivat Chachmei Lublin* (Academy of the Sages of Lublin). For Lublin had been the very spiritual heart of Polish Jewry, renowned for its scholars and sages, one of them so great that he was referred to as the Seer of Lublin.

So important in the life of the entire Polish nation had been the influence of the great Yeshiva of Lublin, that for centuries its rector was appointed by none other than the King of Poland himself. In 1930, 50,000 people, including high-ranking government officials, attended the ceremonies dedicating a new headquarters for the Yeshiva. It was considered to be one of the most modern prewar buildings in all of Poland, six stories high, 120 rooms, a huge auditorium, and even a scale model of the Temple in Jerusalem. In 1939, 500 students studied there full time.

83. Lublin. Building which once housed the great Talmudic Academy. It is now used by the Lublin Medical College.

A horrifying account of the wanton vandalization of this center of learning by the Nazis is found in the *Deutsche Jugendzeitung* (February 1940). "It was a matter of special pride to us," proclaims the Nazi narrator:

> to destroy this Talmudic Academy, known as the greatest in Poland. We threw out of the building the large Talmudic library and brought it to the market place. There, we kindled a fire under the books. The conflagration lasted twenty hours. The Jews of Lublin stood around weeping bitterly. Their outcries rose above our own voices. We summoned a military band, and the triumphant cries of the soldiers drowned out the noise of the wailing Jews.

Today in Lublin, there are only thirty Jews out of the 46,000 who lived there before the war (forty percent of the city's population). Miraculously, the building which housed the famous Yeshiva has survived, and as a center of learning at that. It now houses the Lublin Medical College.

84. Lublin. Last Jewish tailor in a city where, before the war, 97 percent of all tailors were Jews.

85. Lublin. Former Jewish orphanage.

86. *Shames* (sexton) of the only synagogue in Lublin to survive the war.

I asked a professor of the college why there was no memorial of any kind explaining the great historical significance of the building, especially for the future generations of Polish doctors who were unknowingly carrying on the building's reputation as a center for scholarship. Blushing with embarrassment, the good doctor responded, "Rabbi, your question in Poland today is sadly a political one, and I am only a doctor."

Notwithstanding the refusal of the Communist government to memorialize officially this renowned, historic center of scholarship and to include it within the intellectual heritage of the Polish nation, folk legends about the academy and its scholars persist among the people of Lublin. Many of these legends center around the lofty, densely wooded, Grodzisk Hill, near the Yeshiva, where a great stone wall shields a sixteenth-century Jewish burial ground. Here rest not only the academy's most

87. Lublin. Jews' Gate (center, with scaffolding), as seen from the royal castle.

88. Lublin. Plaza where stood the Podzamcze Jewish quarter.

illustrious teachers, but also two of Diaspora Judaism's greatest intellectual giants—Solmon Luria (1501–1573), known by the acronym of *Maharshal* and considered along with *Remo* of Cracow, one of two major architects of contemporary Orthodox Judaism, and Rabbi Meir Lublin (1558–1616), known as the *Maharam.*

A story has been passed down by Polish families who have lived at the foot of this hallowed site for generations, that the sages buried there were so sensitive that even in death their souls required undisturbed silence to continue their eternal studies. After a Catholic monastery was constructed next to the cemetery hill, the legend continues, the monks and rabbinical souls became scholarly neighbors who gloried in meditative silence. When the monastery was converted into a church, however, the cloistered solemnity was shattered by the frequent ringing of a bell. So upset were the departed sages that they pronounced a malediction upon the bell. To this day, we were told, the bell hangs in silence, none daring to ring it for fear of the ancient rabbinical curse.

89. The sole Jew (second from left) in the Lublin market, once predominantly Jewish.

90. Lublin. Polish boy beside scattered bones of Nazi victims in old Jewish cemetery.

91. Lublin. Abandoned memorial to Nazi victims erected by Jewish survivors after the war. In the distance can be seen new housing projects built upon land appropriated from the Jewish cemetery.

While the power of a rabbinical censure may have been effective enough to silence a bell, it had been helpless against a far more deadly sound. While climbing the steep path to the tombs of the *Maharshal* and *Maharam*, we were guided by a Polish teenager to a pit in the cemetery where, protruding through the eroding soil, could be seen the skulls and bones of Lublin Jews massacred there amidst the deafening sounds of Nazi machine-gun fire.

Lublin had been renowned not only as a center of scholarship, of Talmudic sages and academies, but also for a most unusual event which is said to have occurred there in the sixteenth century. At that time, a highly influential Jewish banker by the name of Saul Wahl, for whom a synagogue in the city was named, became, of all things, King of Poland. According to the legend, Saul's father had saved the life of a Polish nobleman, Prince Radziwill, who in gratitude became a patron of Saul. On the day when the election of the new king, Sigismund III, was due for final ratification by the *Sejm* (parliament), Prince Radziwill appointed Saul Wahl to assume the duties of the throne during the interregnum. His reign, however, lasted only one day, as the *Sejm* ratified Sigismund's election before the day's end. Legend or history, the story of Saul Wahl, as part of age-old folklore, testifies to the sense of deep rootedness the Jews felt in Poland.

The Saul Wahl synagogue, and that of the *Maharshal*, which, constructed in 1567, was so huge that it could accommodate 3,000 worshipers, were located at the base of the king's castle. This site became the Jewish quarter referred to as Podzamcze, meaning "below the castle." The location in many ways symbolizes the symbiotic relationship that

92. Lublin resident on park bench by Majdanek.

existed throughout Polish history between the throne and the Jewish community. Wherever in Poland there was a royal castle, one would be sure to find the Jewish quarter nearby.

Podzamcze was a maze of courts and twisting alleys, of houses of study and synagogues of every variety, including the *Kotlerschul*, belonging to the coppersmith guild; the *Mschorsimschul*, for business clerks; the *Lauferschul*, for porters; the *Schneiderschul*, for tailors. This historic section of Lublin was totally leveled by the Nazis. Today, only the former entrance gate, still referred to by the local populace as the Jews' Gate, remains, while Podzamcze ("below the castle") now refers to a vast, empty plaza.

Yeshivat Chachmei Lublin, the *Maharshal*, the Seer of Lublin, Rabbi Meir Lublin . . . were what to Polish Jews had given a city its name. And so it was with Kotsk, Bobov, Ger, Przemysl, Rymanow . . . not seen as merely the names of Polish hamlets, but as great Hasidic courts; not geographical locations, but mystical gateways to the divine.

Hasidism had swept into Poland shortly after its beginnings in the Ukraine in the eighteenth century. By the nineteenth century, it had captured the spirit of more than half of Polish Jewry. The 1648 holocaust and the closing of the Council of Four Lands had sharply curtailed the once vibrant spirit of Polish Talmudic Judaism. It soon became rigid, a dry scholasticism, devoid of emotional content. Such an expression of religion obviously could not meet the needs of masses of persecuted people yearning for comfort and hope. Hasidism's arrival filled the vacuum. It was the greatest religious revival in the long history of the Jewish people. The Hasidic spirit rescued Polish Talmudism from obsolescence, and breathed into it a pulsating life which is still felt by Jews the world over today.

Hasidism focused upon the kabbalistic (mystical) aspects of Judaism. Almost pantheistically, it saw divinity not only in the heavens, but in the forests and pastures of rural Poland as well. Baal Shem Tov, the founder of Hasidism, had discovered his approach while meditating in the forests, and his keynote teaching was that God was omnipresent and immanent: that the question was not where could God be found, but where could He not be; not, was He in the universe, but rather, had we let Him into our hearts?

Hasidism offered a catharsis for the pent-up humiliation and frustration of an oppressed people. It taught that the unsophisticated and simple folk were as important to God in the work of redemption as the elitist rabbinate. Obviously, such an approach to Judaism had a broad appeal to the masses.

Towns and hamlets of Poland were suddenly awakened from insignificance, transformed by the fame of their Hasidic sage into magnetic centers for thousands of fervent pilgrims. Hasidic dynasties, some even with palatial courts, became shrouded in popular folk legend. Esoteric parables, witty maxims, and alleged mystical powers spread the fame of many a *zaddik* (Hasidic master), attracting followers and skeptics alike to his court.

The *zaddik* was seen as a bridge between earth and heaven. His gift from God was the *noblesse oblige* to elevate his fellow humans rung by rung on the kabbalistic ladder of consciousness, and this he often sought to do through ecstatic song and dance, as well as scholarship. In the great halls of the Rebbe's court, sumptuous feats—the Rebbe's *tish* (table)— were held, at which hundreds of anxious devotees hungrily consumed each word of the *zaddik* along with the delectable food, drinking and circle-dancing late into the Polish evenings.

Hasidic courts became veritable centers of poetry, music, and dance, and each melody, approach to life, and even style of dress reflected the personality of the particular *zaddik*. To the Modzhitser Court, for example, flocked famous musicians, Jewish and Gentile alike, to hear the compositions of a *zaddik* who was neither the product of a conservatory nor any other formal musical training, but in whose veins flowed magnificent talent. He is said to have created more than seven hundred different musical compositions; and more than one thousand Hasidim sat at his table every Sabbath to hear his melodies. The musical power of the *zaddikim* remained to the very end, for even on the despairing paths that led to the gas chambers, the soaring Hasidic melodies were often heard, elevating their singers to a realm far above their earthly hell.

The most popular Hasidic dynasty in Poland was found in a town called, of all things, Mount Calvary (Gora Kalwaria); but to Jews, it was Ger, seat of the Gerer Rebbe, the emperor of Polish Hasidism. As great as his accomplishments in learning, so was the Gerer Rebbe's humility, and the masses loved him for it. The story is told that the *zaddik* once wrote a lengthy book and brought it to his teacher and master for review. The sage praised it as a work of absolute genius, rendering totally obsolete the works of all the great sages of the past. The Gerer *zaddik*, concludes the tale, went home and burned the book.

The day before the Sabbath or holidays, additional passenger cars were attached to the train on the route to this village south of Warsaw to accommodate the massive surge of pilgrims seeking out the *zaddik*. Indeed the major industry of the town was providing for the physical and spiritual needs of the pilgrims.

In the summer of 1975, buses ran to Gora Kalwaria, and we had no problems finding a seat. Older Polish residents of the town were quick to point out the former mansion and synagogue of the *zaddik*, but a *zaddik* to them was now only a memory, a word which had entered into the Polish language. A gaping hole in the doorpost where the *mezzuzah* had been was the last sign left that here had been a door to divinity.

The Gerer Rebbe fled to Palestine in 1940, where Phoenix-like he reestablished his court in Jerusalem. Today not one Jew lives in Gora Kalwaria and few ever go there. The *zaddik's* synagogue now serves as a warehouse; his home has been transformed into apartments. Not one tomb is left in the cemetery. Gone forever is Ger, while Gora Kalwaria sinks again into the landscape, just another insignificant hamlet in Poland.

If Ger had been the most popular court in Poland, then Kotsk was the most controversial. The Kotsker pattern of Hasidism was revolutionary, and in many ways contrary to the teachings of Baal Shem Tov. The Kotsker Rebbe, Menahem Mendel, was interested in reaching only an intellectual elite. Whereas classical Hasidism, as exemplified in Ger, was motivated by concern for the masses and emphasized love and compassion, the Kotsker brand was concerned only with the pursuit of intellectual truth. Menahem Mendel demanded constant intellectual struggle, and the zealous militancy of the Hebrew prophets reemerged in Kotsk. While other *zaddikim* soothed and comforted, the Kotsker barked: "As for him who learns Torah and is not deeply troubled by it . . . a very scroundrel is better than he." To a student who once boasted how he had gone through the Talmud, he snapped, "but has the Talmud gone through you?"

Thousands flocked to Kotsk, despite the *zaddik's* often harsh and contemptuous remarks to them. To some, who came in search of miracles, he answered sardonically, "The only miracle I seek to perform is to make a real Hasid," while, to others, he gave advice regarding their business affairs. When asked by a disciple how he knew what advice to offer, being himself far removed from such matters, the Kotsker replied, "From where else can one get the best all-round view of everything?"

No Hasidic Rebbe in Poland antagonized so many other *zaddikim* with his pithy and biting remarks, than the Kotsker, and no *zaddik* so disagreed with the Kotsker's style than Yisakhar Baer of Radoszyce. Between the disciples of these two, quarrels were always in full swing. It took the beloved and venerable *zaddik* of Ger to bring peace between Kotsk and Radoszyce, after the death of Yisakhar Baer. "The world thinks," the Gerer Rebbe taught, "that there was hatred and quarreling

93. Kotsk. Gypsy who now lives in Kotsker Rebbe's home.

between Kotsk and Radoszyce. That is a grave mistake. There was only one difference of opinion: in Kotsk, they aimed to bring the heart of the Jews closer to God; in Radoszyce, they aimed to bring God closer to the heart of the Jews."

A bizarre legend has it that one Friday night Menahem Mendel suddenly pushed aside the *kiddush* cup, blew out the Sabbath candles, and wailed: "There is no judgment, and there is no Judge. Get out of here, you fools. I am neither a rabbi nor the son of a rabbi." For nineteen years after that, until his death, Menahem Mendel secluded himself in his study, living the austere life of an ascetic. Neither his terrifying utterances, however, nor his strange life kept his followers from coming to Kotsk.

No Jews are to be found in Kotsk today, but the legends of the *zaddik* live on among the Polish inhabitants. The Rebbe's wooden home with its odd-shaped cupola still stands. Most of the mansion is now used as a public school, the rest as a haven for gypsies.

The last Kotsker Rabbi, Joseph Morgenstern, is said to have been martyred with his family and followers in 1942. One of his neighbors, Apolonia Rzymoska, seventy-two years old in 1975, recalled

94. Kotsk. Polish neighbor of the last Kotsker Rebbe, murdered in 1942.

him fondly, for the Kotsker Rebbes had mellowed over the years, and the harsh style had given way to the mainstream Hasidic spirit of love and compassion. Apolonia had her grandson take us to where the Kotsker had come to an end, an open pit in the cemetery. There, one could almost still hear the echo of the wail: "There is no judgment, and there is no Judge."

If the court of Ger was the most popular, that of Kotsk the most controversial, and Modrzyce, the most melodious, then Rymanow was perhaps the most beautiful. The Rymanower Rebbe's home and synagogue were considered the most prominent buildings in all the province. The synagogue was a superb example of the unique Jewish architecture of Poland, with its centrally located, supporting pillars, baldachin, cubical form, inward vaulting, and its cavernous interior—a rainbow of polychrome murals, richly carved wood, and wrought-iron artifacts.

Belying all this grandeur and magnificence, the Rymanower Rebbe lived the personal life of an avowed ascetic and mystic. The story is told that during a period when the cost of living was very high, the *zaddik* noticed that his wife was giving smaller loaves of bread to the needy people whom he entertained as guests in his home. He thereupon gave orders to make the loaves larger than before, since loaves were intended to adjust to hunger, not to the price.

During the Napoleonic wars, the Rymanower saw a victory by Napoleon as a harbinger of the coming of the Messiah. One story goes that while baking matzohs for Passover, he prayed long and hard for Napoleon to win, and at that very hour, Napoleon won. Another story has it, however, that when the *zaddik* of Ropczyce, who was visiting the Rymanower that very day, heard this prayer, he wailed, "Oh, I forsee, if it will be so, many Jews will be killed and blood will rise high above our feet."

Tragically, it was the vision of the Ropczycer that ultimately came true. After the Nazis marched into Rymanow in 1942, they sent the entire Jewish population, fifty percent of the town, to their cruel death at

Belzec. Only the Great Synagogue was left standing, in silent vigil, and there it remains today.

In Przemysl, the local weekly newspaper, *Zycie Przemyskie* (Przemysl Life), featured an extremely popular series on the life of their *zaddik*. The articles were interestingly illustrated with many prewar photographs. In the article published the week we were there, the following anecdotes were included:

Once, while sitting in his synagogue, the *zaddik* of Przemysl saw through the window a Jew entering a hallway and eating pork sausage. The indignant rabbi promptly addressed a prayer to God: "Let this house collapse and bury the sinner," he intoned. At that very moment, however, he noticed on the balcony of the building a group of children at play. Feeling sorry for them, the *zaddik* appealed to God not to honor his request. And, lo and behold, it came to pass, miraculously, that the building did not collapse after all.

The *zaddik* once thundered from the pulpit of a Przemysl synagogue against all those who traded on the Sabbath in violation of the religious code. After the service he was approached by an elegantly dressed merchant who handed him a monetary contribution. "Did you find my preaching convincing?" asked the *zaddik*.

"I, personally, did not find it so," the merchant replied, "but I noticed that it made a great impression on the other merchants present. None of them will ever again open his store on the Sabbath. At least, for one day of the week, I will now rid myself of those rascals, my competitors."

As is the case with many anecdotes, this one too, had its roots in real life.

In Radomsko and Nowy Sacz, former famous Hasidic centers, the *zaddikim* of the past do more than linger on in the anecdotes of a local newspaper. Even in death, they still exert magnetic power upon their surviving followers, now scattered throughout the world. The mausole-

95. The Great Synagogue of Nowy Sacz (in Yiddish, Zanz), in the Carpathian Mountains of Galicia. The huge edifice was constructed when this was the court of the famous Zanzer Rebbe. It has remained abandoned since the Jewish community was deported to the Belzec death camp on August 24, 1942.

96. Nowy Sacz. Desecrated Zanzer synagogue interior, once renowned for its polychrome murals. The fern decorations are from Polish scouts, who have been using the building as a club.

97. Last Jews of Nowy Sacz.

ums of these miracle workers survived the war and are watched over by Polish caretakers. For a few zlotys one can step through the bolted steel doors back into the past. There, proof of the *zaddik's* continued influence can be seen in the dozens of paper prayers left by recent pilgrims: Chaim S. from Antwerp seeks the *zaddik's* intervention for his sick wife, Sarah; Moshe P. from Paris desires the Rebbe's aid on a business decision; and from Brooklyn, New York, has come a blank check, made out to the Rebbe, signed by a devotee.

In Bobov, a court famous for its melodies, the Rebbe's synagogue still remains, while his tomb stands a silent, lonely witness on top of a high hill overlooking the idyllic Galician countryside.

In Sokolow, the Rebbe had been famous as a doctor of the body as well as of the soul, writing prescriptions in faultless Latin. The story is told that while the Sokolower Rebbe was celebrating Sukkot, he cried in anguish, "They have killed my son!" At that moment his son, Rabbi Mendel of Wegrow, had been murdered by the Nazis. The brokenhearted

98. Nowy Sacz. *Ohel* of the Zanzer Hasidic dynasty, a shrine built over the *zaddik's* tomb. This was a peculiarly Polish-Jewish custom.

99. Nowy Sacz. *Ohel* interior, showing the tomb (inside fence) of the *zaddik*, Hayim ben Leibush Halberstam (1793-1876), and that of his son Aaron (died 1906) and their disciples. Note the paper supplications from present-day followers scattered around the world.

100. Bobov. Tombs of the Bobowa Hasidic dynasty. The founder, Shlomo Halberstam, was a son of the Zanzer Rebbe.

zaddik died a short time after, being spared the sight of the total destruction of his community, of which today not a trace is to be found.

And so, across the forests and fields of Poland, dozens of hamlets, whose names were once whispered in reverence and awe as gates to the heavens, have sunk into the anonymity of the Polish countryside.

101. Treblinka. A Polish peasant poses by the sign of his village. He remembered when the trains from Warsaw carried human cargo. How could he not, when clouds of human ash and the stench of burning flesh blanketed his village for weeks on end?

102. Treblinka. Stones arranged to symbolize a cemetery deceptively cover the site of the death camp where 800,000 Jews were murdered.

If Ger, Kotsk, Rymanow, Bobov . . . were the gateways to the heavens, Auschwitz, Chelmno, Belzec, Sobibor . . . were the torturous paths to hell. To travel voluntarily to such places is depressing enough, but how in our post-holocaust world is one able to utter the words: "Round trip ticket please . . . to Auschwitz"? The holocaust is so incomprehensible and yet so central to our consciousness that one almost physically shrinks at the mere sound of . . . Auschwitz, Treblinka.

Summer in Treblinka—the phrase itself is a sick joke; summer, nevertheless, does come to Treblinka. Where once agonizing crowds of doomed Jews were herded to their death, forsythia grows and a forest has sprung up. Even songbirds chatter obliviously in this God-forsaken place many hours' journey from Warsaw. Gone are the gas chambers, the crematoria, leaving only a deceptive tranquility. At Treblinka, as at Chelmno, north of Lodz, at Sobibor and at Belzec, the Polish government has sought to blanket the harsh realities of specifically Jewish suffering under the innocuous grass of a memorial park, sterile, clean, a place where one can easily forget, not remember.

103. Entrance to Auschwitz, a brief train-ride from Cracow.

104. Crematoria at Auschwitz, as they were found following the war.

Summer also comes to Auschwitz and Majdanek, but there, the optimism of the sun is harshly reflected by electric fences, stable-like wooden barracks, crematorium chimneys still black from human ash. For at Auschwitz and Majdanek, non-Jewish Poles also perished, and thus the government felt the need to preserve there all the hideous instruments of human slaughter, so that no one will forget. The constant flow of tourists, if such a word can be used for visitors to such a place, is exposed to all the grisly horrors: mountains of human hair, clothes, shoes, the braces and crutches, the heaps of toys, little dolls and teddy bears, the piles of empty gas cans.

The fact that most of the martyrs at Auschwitz and Majdanek were Jews would be hard for the average visitor in the summer of 1975 to perceive. There is a Catholic chapel, but nowhere a Jewish one. There are numerous monuments, plaques, and memorials dedicated to specifically Polish victims, none to Jewish ones. Jews are mentioned—how could they not be?—but buried in endless statistics that most people do not read, like how many eyeglasses, trunks, shoes were found, how much silverware . . .

105. Memorial at Majdanek death camp in the Lublin suburb of Majdan-Tatarski. The monument was designed to symbolize a valley of death, culminating in a massive block of interweaving, irregular forms of stone, resting on two huge monoliths. No mention is made on the memorial of the fact that most of the victims murdered here were Jews. In the distance, between the monoliths, can be seen a huge mausoleum which encompasses a 4,429 cubic-foot mountain of human ash from the camp crematoria.

106. The city of Lublin rises over Majdanek. The Nazis felt no need to conceal the camp from the local populace and the gas chambers are clearly visible from Lublin's main highway.

Before the post-war purges, themselves inconceivable in this land of Auschwitz, some public memorials to the 3,300,000 martyred Jewish Poles were erected by the government. But the granite monuments in Treblinka, Chelmno, and Sobibor, one statue and a bunker in Warsaw, and one thin obelisk in Lublin hardly qualify as a fitting tribute to ten percent of the prewar population. In almost all of those towns where Jews formed the majority, as well as in most cities, there is not so much as even a small plaque to recall the tragic fate of citizens with a thousand-year history of significant contributions to Poland.

This does not mean that the present Polish government has been able to brush aside the past completely. The stench of Treblinka is still too strong in the air. At the height of the purges in 1968, we were told, a macabre ceremony, complete with military pomp and ritual, was conducted before the ghetto memorial in Warsaw on the twenty-fifth anniversary of the uprising. The tragic events of the Nazi era were maliciously twisted on that occasion into a shameless defamation of the Jewish people, both living and dead. None other than Kazimierz Rusinek, Secretary General of the Polish War Veterans, unleashed a vicious attack upon the handful of Jews who remained in Poland, branding them as Zionist conspirators who with other Jews had collaborated with the Nazis during the war.

That such words could be spoken in a post-holocaust era, in a nation where the soil was not yet dry from the blood of millions of murdered Jews, is the real tragedy in the final chapter of the thousand-year saga of Polish Jewry: not so much the crime of desecrated synagogues, nor of vandalized cemeteries and tombs, nor even the shameful lack of memorials or monuments, but, far worse, the unforgivable scapegoating of elderly, helpless people, the broken remnants of the world's most monstrous crimes—denying them even the right to live out the last few years of their anguished lives without fear and senseless suffering.

107. Siedlce. A heap of Jewish tombstones, all that remains of a community which once numbered 15,000.

Writing in *The New York Times* (International edition, October 23, 1965), A.M. Rosenthal, who covered the Warsaw ceremonies on the occasion of the twenty-fifth anniversary of the Ghetto uprising, wrote:

> To the measure that the Jews of the ghetto died to save future Polish Jews from anti-Semitism in Poland, to that measure they died in vain. . . . Those Jews who died in the ghetto had lived their lives amidst the heavy stench of Polish anti-Semitism, that stench is lighter now and again perfumed with guilt, but I believe it still hangs over Poland like a miasma.

Bibliography

Research for this project was carried out at the YIVO Library in New York City, the Yad Vashem Library in Jerusalem, and the Jewish Historical Institute in Warsaw. Among the chief sources used were the "Books of Memory" of Polish cities and towns, published in Yiddish and Hebrew by the various survivor associations in Israel and around the world. These works, too numerous to list here, are reminiscences of prewar Jewish life in Poland and include locations of synagogues and communal institutions which existed prior to 1939. All this information has served as an invaluable guide in helping to trace the remnants of Jewish existence as they survive on the contemporary scene.

In addition, the author has further consulted the following books:

Jacob Apenszlak: *The Black Book of Polish Jewry*, Roy Publishers, New York, 1943.

David Davidowicz: *Batay knesset ba-polen v-charvotam* [The Synagogues of Poland and their Destruction], Mosad Harav Kook and Yad Vashem, Jerusalem, 1960.

S. Markovich Dubnow: *History of the Jews in Russia and Poland*, Translated from the Russian by I. Friedlander, Jewish Publication Society, Philadelphia, 1916–20.

Encyclopaedia Hebraica, Encyclopaedia Publishing House, Jerusalem, 1967.

Encyclopaedia Judaica, Keter Publishing House, Jerusalem, 1972.

Israel Heilperin: *Bate Yisroel ba-polen* [The Household of Israel in Poland (From the Beginning Days until the Holocaust)], Zionist Organization of Israel, Jerusalem, 1948.

George Lukomski: *Jewish Art in European Synagogues*, Hutchinson & Co., London, 1947.

Peter Meyer, Bernard Weinryb, et al.: *The Jews in the Soviet Satellites*, Syracuse University Press, Syracuse, 1953.

Bernard Weinryb: *The Jews of Poland: A Social and Economic History from 1100 to 1800*, Jewish Publication Society, Philadelphia, 1973.